THE TRUTH ON
GOD'S PERSPECTIVE
ON BEING WEALTHY

BY STEVEN ANTHONY SPENCER

The Truth on
GOD'S PERSPECTIVE
on Being Wealthy

By:

STEVEN ANTHONY SPENCER

TABLE OF CONTENTS

INTRODUCTION

Thank you sincerely for choosing to invest in this book. Your decision today marks the beginning of a transformative journey. As you delve into these pages, be prepared for a paradigm shift in your understanding of finances. I am confident that by the end of this read, your approach to wealth and financial stewardship will be revolutionized, ensuring that your financial life will never be the same again. Embrace the change, and let the journey begin!

"For the love of money is a root of all kinds of evil. Some people, eager for money, have wandered from the faith and pierced themselves with many griefs."

1 Timothy 6:10 (NIV)

This verse cautions against the love of money and underscores the spiritual implications of prioritizing wealth over faith. It provides insight into the balance and discernment needed when navigating the realm of prosperity from a divine perspective.

Biblical financial principles, at their core, revolve around a few foundational tenets that offer profound insights yet are simple to grasp. First and foremost is the principle of stewardship. The Bible teaches that everything we possess, including our finances, is not truly ours but belongs to God. We are merely stewards of these resources. In practical terms, this means we should manage our money with a sense of responsibility, acknowledging that we're accountable to a higher power. This perspective shifts our view from ownership to guardianship, fostering a more responsible and thoughtful approach to spending, saving, and giving.

Another fundamental biblical financial principle is the virtue of contentment. In a world driven by consumerism and a constant desire for more, the Bible advises against the love of money and emphasizes the importance of being content with what we have. The Apostle Paul, in his letters, often highlighted that true contentment comes not from material abundance but from inner peace and a strong relationship with God. This doesn't mean that ambition or the desire to improve one's financial situation is wrong. Instead, it reminds us not to let the pursuit of wealth become our primary focus, overshadowing our spiritual and moral well-being.

Lastly, the Bible places a significant emphasis on generosity and caring for the less fortunate. Verses from both the Old and New Testaments advocate for giving to the poor, helping those in need, and not hoarding riches. The principle here is clear: blessings, including financial ones, are given not just for personal benefit but to be a blessing to others. By giving tithes, offerings, or just helping someone in need, we're not just doing a good deed; we're aligning our financial practices with divine principles of love, compassion, and communal well-being.

CHAPTER 1:
THE SOURCE OF ALL WEALTH

"But remember the LORD your God, for it is He who gives you the ability to produce wealth, and so confirms His covenant, which He swore to your ancestors, as it is today."

-**Deuteronomy 8:18** (NIV)

According to the Word of God, all wealth and abundance originate from the Divine. Scriptures across various religious traditions affirm that the Earth and its bounties are God's creations, given to humanity as a testament to His benevolence. In the Judeo-Christian tradition, passages from the Bible, such as Deuteronomy 8:18, remind believers that it is God "who gives you the power to get wealth." This perspective underscores the idea that while humans may labor and strive, it is ultimately God's grace and will that bestow prosperity upon them. Recognizing the divine as the true source of all wealth instills a sense of humility and gratitude, urging individuals to use their resources wisely and righteously.

"The earth is the Lord's, and everything in it, the world, and all who live in it."

- **Psalm 24:1** (NIV)

Certainly, the Bible is rich with verses that highlight God's providence and care for His creation. Here are three verses that support this theme:

"And my God will meet all your needs according to the riches of his glory in Christ Jesus."

- **Philippians 4:19** (NIV)

"Look at the birds of the air; they do not sow or reap or store away in barns, and yet your heavenly Father feeds them. Are you not much more valuable than they?"

 - **Matthew 6:26** (NIV)

"But seek first his kingdom and his righteousness, and all these things will be given to you as well."

 - **Matthew 6:33** (NIV)

These verses emphasize the unwavering care and provision of God, assuring believers of His commitment to meet their needs and guide their paths.

CHAPTER 2:
WEALTH AS A BLESSING AND A TEST

Here are two Bible verses that support the theme of wealth being both a blessing and a test:

1. "The LORD has blessed my master abundantly, and he has become wealthy. He has given him sheep and cattle, silver and gold, male and female servants, and camels and donkeys."

  - **Genesis 24:35 (NIV)**

This verse exemplifies wealth as a blessing from God, bestowed upon those whom He favors.

2. "Those who want to get rich fall into temptation and a trap and into many foolish and harmful desires that plunge people into ruin and destruction."

  - **1 Timothy 6:9 (NIV)**

This verse speaks to the testing nature of wealth, highlighting the potential pitfalls and temptations that can accompany the pursuit of riches.

Together, these verses give a holistic view of wealth, illustrating its dual nature as both a divine favor and a spiritual challenge.

A Bible verse that supports the idea of wealth as a blessing from God is:

"The blessing of the LORD brings wealth, without painful toil for it."

- **Proverbs 10:22 (NIV)**

This verse underscores the idea that true, meaningful wealth comes as a direct blessing from the LORD and is not just the result of mere human effort.

Here are three Bible verses that highlight the responsibilities that come with wealth:

1. "Whoever can be trusted with very little can also be trusted with much, and whoever is dishonest with very little will also be dishonest with much. So, if you have not been trustworthy in handling worldly wealth, who will trust you with true riches?"

   - **Luke 16:10-11** (NIV)

This verse underscores the principle of stewardship, emphasizing the idea that how one manages wealth reflects their character and trustworthiness.

2. "Command those who are rich in this present world not to be arrogant nor to put their hope in wealth, which is so uncertain, but to put their hope in God, who richly provides us with everything for our enjoyment. Command them to do good, to be rich in good deeds, and to be generous and willing to share."

   - **1 Timothy 6:17-18** (NIV)

 Here, the responsibilities of the wealthy are outlined, emphasizing humility, generosity, and the importance of grounding one's hope in God rather than material wealth.

3. "Give to everyone who asks you, and if anyone takes what belongs to you, do not demand it back."

   - **Luke 6:30** (NIV)

This verse speaks to the importance of generosity and the responsibility to share one's resources with those in need.

These verses provide insights into the biblical perspective on the duties and moral imperatives that come with possessing wealth.

CHAPTER 3:
THE DANGERS OF RICHES

There are at least three Bible verses that delve into the dangers and challenges associated with riches:

1. **"Then Jesus said to his disciples, 'Truly I tell you; it is hard for someone who is rich to enter the kingdom of heaven. Again, I tell you, it is easier for a camel to go through the eye of a needle than for someone who is rich to enter the kingdom of God.'"**

   - **Matthew 19:23-24** (NIV)

This passage speaks to the spiritual challenges wealth can pose, suggesting that riches might become an impediment to one's relationship with God.

2. **"Those who trust in their riches will fall, but the righteous will thrive like a green leaf."**

   - **Proverbs 11:28** (NIV)

This verse contrasts the transient nature of wealth with the enduring virtue of righteousness, cautioning against placing one's trust solely in material wealth.

3. **"Do not wear yourself out to get rich; do not trust your own cleverness. Cast but a glance at riches, and they are gone, for they will surely sprout wings and fly off to the sky like an eagle."**

   - **Proverbs 23:4-5** (NIV)

This proverbial wisdom warns of the fleeting nature of riches and advises against exhausting oneself in the sole pursuit of wealth.

These verses provide a sobering perspective on the potential pitfalls of wealth and the spiritual discernment required when navigating its challenges.

A Bible verse that provides a clear warning against hoarding and the love of money is:

"Do not store up for yourselves treasures on earth, where moths and vermin destroy, and where thieves break in and steal. But store up for yourselves treasures in heaven, where moths and vermin do not destroy, and where thieves do not break in and steal. For where your treasure is, there your heart will be also."

- **Matthew 6:19-21** (NIV)

This passage not only speaks against hoarding material possessions but also emphasizes the importance of valuing spiritual riches over earthly treasures. It serves as a reminder that the true location of one's "treasure" indicates the orientation of one's heart.

The parable of the rich man and Lazarus, found in the Gospel of Luke, is a profound biblical narrative illustrating the dangers of wealth when paired with indifference. The story unfolds with a wealthy man who lived in luxury, while at his gate lay Lazarus, a poor man, longing for mere scraps from the rich man's table. Both men eventually died; Lazarus was carried to Abraham's side, a place of comfort, whereas the rich man found himself in torment. When the rich man pleaded for relief, Abraham reminded him of the life he lived in luxury while ignoring Lazarus in his suffering. This parable serves as a stark reminder that wealth, when coupled with neglect for the needy, can have eternal consequences, emphasizing the moral responsibility that comes with abundance.

A Bible verse that highlights the potential for wealth to lead one astray is:

"No one can serve two masters. Either you will hate the one and love the other, or you will be devoted to the one and despise the other. You cannot serve both God and money."

- **Matthew 6:24** (NIV)

This verse emphasizes the conflict between the pursuit of wealth and serving God, suggesting that the two can often be at odds with one another, and that devotion to money can divert one from a righteous path.

One of the most poignant biblical narratives illustrating the pitfalls of riches is the story of the rich young ruler. In the Gospels (for example, in **Mark 10:17-27**), a wealthy young man approaches Jesus and inquiries about inheriting eternal life. Jesus tells him to follow the commandments, to which the young man confidently replies he has done since his youth. Seeing this, Jesus then advises him to sell all he has, give to the poor, and follow Him. The young man's face falls, and he leaves sorrowfully, for he had great possessions. Jesus then remarks on how hard it is for the wealthy to enter the kingdom of God, comparing it to a camel trying to go through the eye of a needle. This narrative vividly captures the challenges riches can pose to one's spiritual journey, illustrating the tension between earthly attachments and divine aspirations.

CHAPTER 4:
GENEROSITY AND GIVING

Here are two Bible verses that emphasize the importance of generosity and giving:

1. "Each of you should give what you have decided in your heart to give, not reluctantly or under compulsion, for God loves a cheerful giver."

  - **2 Corinthians 9:7 (NIV)**

2. "Give, and it will be given to you. A good measure, pressed down, shaken together and running over, will be poured into your lap. For with the measure you use, it will be measured to you."

  - **Luke 6:38 (NIV)**

Both verses underscore the blessings and virtues associated with selfless giving and encourage believers to cultivate a generous spirit.

The Bible, especially in the Old Testament, provides specific instructions and principles regarding tithes and offerings. Here's a summary of some of the key verses:

1. **Leviticus 27:30-32 (NIV):**

  > **"A tithe of everything from the land, whether grain from the soil or fruit from the trees, belongs to the LORD; it is holy to the LORD. Whoever would redeem any of their tithe must add a fifth of the value to it. Every tithe of the herd and flock—every tenth animal that passes under the shepherd's rod—will be holy to the LORD."**

This establishes the principle of giving one-tenth (a tithe) of one's produce or livestock to the Lord.

2. **Deuteronomy 14:22-29** (NIV):

In this passage, the Israelites are instructed to set aside a tenth of their produce each year and, if they lived too far from the place the Lord chose for worship, to convert their tithe into silver. They were then to use that silver to buy whatever they liked and eat in the presence of the Lord. Additionally, every third year, the tithe was to be stored locally and used to support the Levites, strangers, orphans, and widows.

3. **Malachi 3:8-10** (NIV):

> "Will a mere mortal rob God? Yet you rob me. But you ask, 'How are we robbing you?' In tithes and offerings. You are under a curse—your whole nation—because you are robbing me. Bring the whole tithe into the storehouse, so that there may be food in my house. Test me in this," says the LORD Almighty, "and see if I will not throw open the floodgates of heaven and pour out so much blessing that there will not be room enough to store it."

This is a powerful passage where God challenges the people to be faithful in their tithing, promising blessings in return.

4. **2 Corinthians 9:6-7** (NIV):

> "Remember this: Whoever sows sparingly will also reap sparingly, and whoever sows generously will also reap generously. Each of you should give what you have decided in your heart to give, not reluctantly or under compulsion, for God loves a cheerful giver."

While this New Testament passage does not explicitly mention tithing, it speaks to the principle of generous giving and the blessings that follow.

These verses, among others, illuminate the biblical perspective on tithes and offerings, emphasizing the importance of giving back to God a portion of what He has blessed us with and supporting the work of His kingdom.

CHAPTER 5:
ETHICAL EARNINGS

The Bible provides guidelines on ethical behavior, including principles on acquiring and managing wealth. Here are three verses that underscore the importance of ethical earnings:

1. **Proverbs 16:8** (NIV):

> "Better a little with righteousness than much gain with injustice."

This verse emphasizes the value of earning honestly, even if the gains are modest, over acquiring wealth through unethical means.

2. **Proverbs 13:11** (NIV):

> "Dishonest money dwindles away, but whoever gathers money little by little makes it grow."

This wisdom from Proverbs indicates that wealth accumulated through deceitful means won't last, but ethical, diligent work leads to sustainable prosperity.

3. **Jeremiah 22:13** (NIV):

> "Woe to him who builds his palace by unrighteousness, his upper rooms by injustice, making his own people work for nothing, not paying them for their labor."

Through the prophet Jeremiah, God condemns exploitation and the withholding of fair wages. The verse underscores the importance of treating workers justly and providing fair compensation for their labor.

These verses highlight the biblical imperative to ensure that one's earnings are grounded in righteousness and fairness.

The Bible has numerous verses that address the importance of just economic practices and highlight prohibitions against exploitation, usury, and fraud. Here are three verses that speak directly to these issues:

1. **Exodus 22:25** (NIV):

> "If you lend money to one of my people among you who is needy, do not treat it like a business deal; charge no interest."

This commandment speaks against usury, particularly emphasizing the importance of not charging interest to those who are already financially vulnerable.

2. **Leviticus 19:13** (NIV):

> "Do not defraud or rob your neighbor. Do not hold back the wages of a hired worker overnight."

Here, the prohibition is clear against both defrauding someone (which would encompass a range of exploitative and dishonest practices) and withholding wages unjustly from workers.

3. **Proverbs 11:1** (NIV):

> "The LORD detests dishonest scales, but accurate weights find favor with him."

This proverb warns against fraudulent practices in business, using the metaphor of "dishonest scales," which would have been a direct reference to cheating in trade during biblical times.

All these verses underscore God's desire for ethical and just practices in business and personal dealings, emphasizing the importance of fairness, honesty, and compassion.

Certainly, the Bible provides principles for conducting business with integrity and ethics. Here are two verses that emphasize ethical practices in business and trade:

1. **Leviticus 19:35-36** (NIV):

> "Do not use dishonest standards when measuring length, weight, or quantity. Use honest scales and honest weights, an honest ephah and an honest him. I am the LORD your God, who brought you out of Egypt."

This passage emphasizes the importance of honesty in trade, especially in the measurements and standards used, which was crucial in ancient trade practices.

2. **Proverbs 20:23** (NIV):

> "The LORD detests differing weights, and dishonest scales do not please him."

Again, using the metaphor of scales, this proverb underscores the divine displeasure with deceitful business practices and emphasizes the value God places on honesty and integrity in all dealings.

These verses highlight the biblical guidance for ensuring ethical conduct, especially in the realm of business and trade.

CHAPTER 6:
THE SPIRITUAL PERSPECTIVE ON WEALTH

Certainly, the Bible provides insights into the spiritual perspective on wealth, offering both warnings and wisdom. Here are three verses that touch upon this theme:

1. **Matthew 6:21** (NIV):

> "For where your treasure is, there your heart will be also."

Jesus, in this passage, highlights the profound connection between one's treasures (or wealth) and one's heart. It's a reminder that what we value materially can have spiritual implications.

2. **1 Timothy 6:10** (NIV):

> "For the love of money is a root of all kinds of evil. Some people, eager for money, have wandered from the faith and pierced themselves with many griefs."

This verse offers a cautionary note on the dangers of prioritizing wealth over spiritual matters. It's not the money itself, but the love of it that poses spiritual risks.

3. **Proverbs 11:28** (NIV):

> "Whoever trusts in his riches will fall, but the righteous will thrive like a green leaf."

This proverb juxtaposes the folly of placing one's ultimate trust in wealth against the flourishing of the righteous. It underscores the ephemeral nature of material wealth compared to spiritual integrity.

Together, these verses provide a nuanced view on wealth from a spiritual perspective, emphasizing the importance of aligning material resources with spiritual values.

The Bible offers various insights regarding the transient nature of worldly riches. Here are two verses that succinctly convey this theme:

1. **Matthew 6:19-20** (NIV):

> "Do not store up for yourselves treasures on earth, where moths and vermin destroy, and where thieves break in and steal. But store up for yourselves treasures in heaven, where moths and vermin do not destroy, and where thieves do not break in and steal."

Jesus, in His Sermon on the Mount, contrasts the fleeting nature of earthly wealth with the enduring value of heavenly treasures, encouraging His followers to seek the latter.

2. **Proverbs 23:4-5** (NIV):

> "Do not wear yourself out to get rich; do not trust your own cleverness. Cast but a glance at riches, and they are gone, for they will surely sprout wings and fly off to the sky like an eagle."

This Proverb vividly depicts the transient nature of wealth, warning against the futile pursuit of riches and reminding readers of the temporary nature of material wealth.

These verses teach the principle that worldly riches are not permanent and emphasize the importance of focusing on eternal values.

The Bible offers a rich tapestry of teachings on the concept of true wealth, emphasizing that what's valued in God's eyes often contrasts with worldly views on wealth. Here are three verses reflecting this theme:

1. **Luke 12:15** (NIV):

 > "Then he said to them, 'Watch out! Be on your guard against all kinds of greed; life does not consist in an abundance of possessions.'"

In this passage, Jesus cautions against measuring life's worth by the accumulation of material possessions, stressing the deeper, more intrinsic values.

2. **Proverbs 22:1** (NIV):

 > "A good name is more desirable than great riches; to be esteemed is better than silver or gold."

This proverb emphasizes the value of a good reputation and integrity over and above material wealth, highlighting what's truly precious in the eyes of God.

3. **Matthew 6:33** (NIV):

 > "But seek first his kingdom and his righteousness, and all these things will be given to you as well."

Jesus teaches the principle of prioritizing the pursuit of God's kingdom and righteousness above all else. In doing so, one discovers the true wealth and provision that God offers.

These verses underscore that in God's perspective, true wealth is not just about material accumulation, but more about the state of one's heart, character, and spiritual alignment.

Certainly, one of the Bible verses that aptly emphasizes the significance of spiritual growth over material accumulation is:

Matthew 16:26 (NIV):

> "What good will it be for someone to gain the whole world, yet forfeit their soul? Or what can anyone give in exchange for their soul?"

This verse, spoken by Jesus, underscores the immeasurable value of one's soul and spiritual well-being compared to the fleeting nature of worldly gains. The rhetorical questions posed emphasize the idea that no material wealth can be deemed equivalent to the worth of a person's soul.

The Truth on God's Perspective on Being Wealthy

rhetorical questions posed emphasize the idea that no material wealth can be deemed equivalent to the worth of a person's soul.

CHAPTER 7:
STEWARDSHIP AND RESPONSIBILITY

The concept of stewardship and responsibility runs throughout the Bible, emphasizing that everything belongs to God and humans are entrusted to manage and care for His creation responsibly. Here are three verses that illuminate this theme:

1. **Genesis 2:15** (NIV):

> "The Lord God took the man and put him in the Garden of Eden to work it and take care of it."

This verse underscores humanity's initial role as caretakers and stewards of God's creation, highlighting the responsibility given to man to maintain and protect the environment.

2. **1 Corinthians 4:2** (NIV):

> "Now it is required that those who have been given trust must prove faithful."

Paul, in this verse, speaks to the importance of faithfulness in stewardship. Whether it's about spiritual gifts, opportunities, or material resources, those entrusted with them are expected to handle them with faithfulness.

3. **Luke 12:48b** (NIV):

> "From everyone who has been given much, much will be demanded; and from the one who has been entrusted with much, much more will be asked."

Jesus, in this parable, emphasizes the responsibility that comes with blessings and resources. The greater the gifts and resources one has, the greater the expectation for their responsible and benevolent use.

Together, these verses paint a picture of God's expectation for humanity to be responsible stewards, not just of material resources, but of all the blessings and opportunities He bestows.

The Bible provides clear guidance on using wealth in ways that are in line with divine principles and purposes. Here are three verses that emphasize this responsibility:

1. **Proverbs 3:9** (NIV):

> "Honor the LORD with your wealth, with the first fruits of all your crops;"

This verse speaks to the idea of giving the best portion of what we earn back to God, demonstrating trust in Him and acknowledging Him as the source of all blessings.

2. **1 Timothy 6:17-18** (NIV):

> "Command those who are rich in this present world not to be arrogant nor to put their hope in wealth, which is so uncertain, but to put their hope in God, who richly provides us with everything for our enjoyment. Command them to do good, to be rich in good deeds, and to be generous and willing to share."

In this guidance from Paul to Timothy, there's a call for those with wealth to approach it with humility, to do good with it, and to be generous, reflecting the heart of God.

3. **Matthew 25:40** (NIV):

> "The King will reply, 'Truly I tell you, whatever you did for one of the least of these brothers and sisters of mine, you did for me.'"

While this verse is from the parable of the sheep and the goats, it underscores the principle that how we use our resources (including wealth) to help others, especially the vulnerable, is a direct reflection of our service to God.

These verses collectively emphasize that wealth, while a blessing, carries with it the responsibility to be used in ways that honor God, benefit others, and align with divine principles.

The Bible offers practical guidance on how to manage and distribute wealth responsibly, emphasizing principles of wisdom, generosity, and justice. Here are three verses that illuminate this theme:

1. **Proverbs 13:22** (NIV):

> "A good person leaves an inheritance for their children's children, but a sinner's wealth is stored up for the righteous."

This verse stresses the value of long-term financial planning and the importance of considering future generations. It's a reminder of the responsibility to manage and distribute wealth with foresight and care.

2. **2 Corinthians 9:6-7** (NIV):

> "Remember this: Whoever sows sparingly will also reap sparingly, and whoever sows generously will also reap generously. Each of you should give what you have decided in your heart to give, not reluctantly or under compulsion, for God loves a cheerful giver."

In this passage, Paul encourages believers in Corinth to give generously, emphasizing the principle of sowing and reaping. It's a lesson in both generosity and the attitude with which one should distribute wealth.

3. **Proverbs 11:24-25** (NIV):

> "One person gives freely, yet gains even more; another withholds unduly, but comes to poverty. A generous person will prosper; whoever refreshes others will be refreshed."

This proverb highlights the paradox that those who give generously often find themselves blessed in return. It offers practical guidance on the positive outcomes of distributing wealth with a generous heart.

These verses reflect the biblical principles on managing and distributing wealth, offering insights into the balance of wise stewardship and compassionate generosity.

CHAPTER 8:
THE ROLE OF CONTENTMENT

The Bible emphasizes the importance of contentment and the peace that comes from finding sufficiency in God rather than external circumstances. Here are two verses that underscore this principle:

1. **Philippians 4:11-12** (NIV):

> "I am not saying this because I am in need, for I have learned to be content whatever the circumstances. I know what it is to be in need, and I know what it is to have plenty. I have learned the secret of being content in any and every situation, whether well fed or hungry, whether living in plenty or in want."

In this passage, the Apostle Paul writes from a place of personal experience, highlighting that contentment is not based on external situations but on an internal perspective shaped by faith.

2. **1 Timothy 6:6** (NIV):

> "But godliness with contentment is great gain."

In his letter to Timothy, Paul emphasizes that the true gain in life is not found in accumulating possessions or wealth, but in pursuing a life of godliness accompanied by a contented heart.

Both verses suggest that genuine contentment is a profound inner state of peace and satisfaction that is not dependent on external factors but is rooted in one's relationship with God.

The Bible consistently emphasizes the importance of gratitude, recognizing blessings, and appreciating what one has. Here are four verses that underscore this theme:

1. **Psalm 118:24** (NIV):

> "This is the day the Lord has made; let us rejoice and be glad in it."

This psalm serves as a reminder to be grateful for every day given by God and to find joy in the present moment.

2. **1 Thessalonians 5:18** (NIV):

> "Give thanks in all circumstances; for this is God's will for you in Christ Jesus."

Paul's exhortation to the Thessalonians reminds believers to maintain a grateful attitude regardless of their circumstances, recognizing God's hand and purpose in all things.

3. **James 1:17** (NIV):

> "Every good and perfect gift is from above, coming down from the Father of the heavenly lights, who does not change like shifting shadows."

James points out that all blessings, both big and small, are gifts from God, prompting believers to appreciate and acknowledge their source.

4. **Proverbs 15:16** (NIV):

> "Better a little with the fear of the Lord than great wealth with turmoil."

This proverb emphasizes the value of spiritual peace and contentment over material wealth, encouraging appreciation of what one has, even if it seems modest in comparison to others.

These verses collectively encourage believers to cultivate a heart of gratitude, to recognize their blessings, and to appreciate the gifts they've been given, irrespective of size or worldly value.

The Bible offers several warnings about the dangers of greed and the pitfalls of constantly comparing oneself to others. Here are three verses that highlight these themes:

1. **Luke 12:15** (NIV):

> "Then he said to them, 'Watch out! Be on your guard against all kinds of greed; life does not consist in an abundance of possessions.'"

In this passage, Jesus warns His listeners about the dangers of greed, emphasizing that the true essence of life isn't found in material possessions.

2. **Proverbs 28:25** (NIV):

> "The greedy stir up conflict, but those who trust in the LORD will prosper."

This Proverb suggests that greed can lead to conflict and discord, whereas placing trust in the Lord leads to prosperity in a holistic and spiritual sense.

3. **2 Corinthians 10:12** (NIV):

> "We do not dare to classify or compare ourselves with some who commend themselves. When they measure themselves by themselves and compare themselves with themselves, they are not wise."

Here, the Apostle Paul warns against the folly of self-comparison, especially when it's based on worldly standards. The verse indicates that wisdom lies in not measuring one's worth by comparing oneself to others.

These verses collectively emphasize the spiritual dangers associated with greed and the pitfalls of basing one's value on comparisons with others. They encourage contentment, gratitude, and finding worth in one's relationship with God rather than material possessions or societal standards.

The Bible provides wisdom on how to cultivate contentment amidst the distractions and desires of a materialistic world. Here are four verses that offer strategies and insights into nurturing a contented heart:

1. **Matthew 6:19-21** (NIV):

> "Do not store up for yourselves treasures on earth, where moths and vermin destroy, and where thieves break in and steal. But store up for yourselves treasures in heaven, where moths and vermin do not destroy, and where thieves do not break in and steal. For where your treasure is, there your heart will be also."

Jesus emphasizes the importance of valuing eternal treasures over temporary, earthly ones, directing our focus and affections on what truly lasts.

2. **Philippians 4:11-12** (NIV):

> "I am not saying this because I am in need, for I have learned to be content whatever the circumstances. I know what it is to be in need, and I know what it is to have plenty. I have learned the secret of being content in any and every situation, whether well fed or hungry, whether living in plenty or in want."

The Apostle Paul discusses his personal journey to contentment, suggesting that it is a learned attitude, independent of external circumstances.

3. **Hebrews 13:5** (NIV):

> "Keep your lives free from the love of money and be content with what you have, because God has said, 'Never will I leave you; never will I forsake you.'"

This verse underscores the importance of valuing God's constant presence and faithfulness over material possessions, highlighting the security that comes from a relationship with Him.

4. **Colossians 3:2** (NIV):

> "Set your minds on things above, not on earthly things."

Paul advises the believers in Colossae to shift their focus from the material world to the spiritual realm, aligning their priorities with God's kingdom.

Collectively, these verses provide strategies for contentment, emphasizing the prioritization of spiritual values, recognizing the transient nature of material possessions, and finding satisfaction in God's enduring presence and promises.

CHAPTER 9:
SEEKING DIVINE GUIDANCE

Certainly. Here are four prayers that individuals can utilize when seeking God's guidance in matters related to wealth and financial decisions:

1. **Prayer for Wisdom in Financial Decisions**:

> "Heavenly Father, you are the source of all wisdom and understanding. As I face financial decisions and choices about wealth, I humbly seek Your guidance. Illuminate my path and help me discern what aligns with Your will. Grant me the prudence to manage my resources in a manner that honors You and blesses those around me. In Jesus' name, I pray. Amen."

2. **Prayer for Contentment and Avoidance of Greed**:

> "Lord Almighty, in a world that constantly urges me to desire more, help me find contentment in what I have. Keep my heart free from the love of money and teach me to find true riches in Your presence and in serving others. Let me always value eternal treasures over fleeting material gains. Guide my steps and keep me from greed. In Your name, I pray. Amen."

3. **Prayer for Generosity and Stewardship**:

> "Gracious God, thank You for the blessings and resources You've entrusted to me. Instill in me a heart of generosity, that I may use what I must bless others and further Your kingdom. Teach me to be a good steward of my wealth, using it for righteous purposes and in ways that echo Your love and compassion. Guide me in my giving, investing, and spending. In Jesus' name, I pray. Amen."

4. **Prayer for Trust in God's Provision**:

> "Father, in times of financial uncertainty or when faced with difficult decisions regarding my wealth, I choose to trust in Your unending provision. You have always provided for my needs and cared for me. Help me to remember Your faithfulness, even when I cannot see the way forward. Lead me in paths of righteousness, and let my trust always be rooted in You, my Provider and Sustainer. Amen."

These prayers are designed to help believers approach wealth and financial matters with a heart aligned to God's will, seeking His wisdom and direction in all things.

The Bible contains numerous accounts of individuals who sought divine direction concerning their wealth or resources. One notable account is of Solomon, the King of Israel. When God appeared to Solomon in a dream and offered him anything he desired, instead of asking for wealth, long life, or the death of his enemies, Solomon asked for wisdom to govern God's people rightly. In response to this selfless request, God granted him unparalleled wisdom and blessed him with immense wealth and honor.

From **1 Kings 3:9-13** (NIV):

>"So, give your servant a discerning heart to govern your people and to distinguish between right and wrong. For who can govern this great people of yours?" The Lord was pleased that Solomon had asked for this. So, God said to him, "Since you have asked for this and not for long life or wealth for yourself, nor have asked for the death of your enemies but for discernment in administering justice, I will do what you have asked. I will give you a wise and discerning heart, so that there will never be anyone like you, nor will there ever be. Moreover, I will give you what you have not asked for—both wealth and honor—so that in your lifetime you will have no equal among kings."

This account underscores the idea that when individuals prioritize divine wisdom and righteousness in their pursuits, God may bless them abundantly, both with spiritual insights and material wealth.

CHAPTER 10:
REAL TESTIMONIALS

1. **Pastor Rick Warren:**

Rick Warren, the respected author of "The Purpose Driven Life" and the senior pastor of Saddleback Church in California, has consistently demonstrated an alignment of his personal wealth with biblical teachings. Following the immense success of his book, which has sold tens of millions of copies worldwide, Warren adopted a reverse tithe, choosing to donate 90% of his income and live on the remaining 10%. Furthermore, he returned his salary from the past 25 years to the church. This action by Warren exemplifies the scripture found in Matthew 6:21, "For where your treasure is, there your heart will be also." Warren's actions indicate a genuine commitment to prioritize heavenly rewards over earthly possessions [1].

2. **Pastor John Wesley:**

The 18th-century theologian and founder of the Methodist movement, John Wesley, epitomized a biblically grounded approach to wealth. Wesley's principle regarding money was simple: "Earn all you can, save all you can, and give all you can." Even when his publications brought him considerable income, Wesley lived modestly, directing most of his earnings to advance the gospel, fund educational projects, and assist the underprivileged. This aligns with Paul's warning in 1 Timothy 6:10, emphasizing that it's the "love of money" that poses spiritual dangers, not the money itself. Wesley's life serves as a testament to this principle [2].

3. **Pastor David Platt**:

Author of the book "Radical" and a prominent voice in contemporary Christian leadership, David Platt frequently challenges Christians to reassess their views on wealth in the context of the Bible. Personally, Platt champions a life of simplicity, channeling his resources to global missions and addressing issues such as extreme poverty and human trafficking. This commitment mirrors James 1:27, which defines true religion as caring for the "orphans and widows in their distress." Through his lifestyle and teachings, Platt emphasizes the significance of using wealth to further the kingdom of God over pursuing personal luxury [3].

LESSON LEARNED and INSIGHTS GAINED from their EXPERIENCE:

1. **Pastor Rick Warren**:

Rick Warren, the esteemed author of "The Purpose Driven Life" and leader of the Saddleback Church, consistently emphasizes the transient nature of earthly possessions. From his unexpected success, he learned firsthand the dangers and distractions that significant wealth can bring. However, rather than becoming ensnared, Warren chose a lifestyle of generosity, often pointing out that true fulfillment doesn't come from material accumulation but from purpose and service to others. His life is a testament to the idea that true wealth lies not in what we keep but in what we give away [1].

2. **Pastor John Wesley**:

John Wesley's experiences with wealth taught him the importance of disciplined stewardship. His mantra about earning, saving, and giving was not just a theological stance but was borne out of observing the socio-economic challenges of his time. He learned that money, while morally neutral, can exert a powerful influence over one's life. To counteract its potentially negative effects, Wesley promoted a disciplined approach to finances that prioritized generosity and frugality, insisting that the love of God and neighbor should guide one's financial decisions [2].

3. **Pastor David Platt**:

David Platt's journey, particularly articulated in his book "Radical," underscores the stark contrast between the Western Christian's relationship with wealth and the teachings of Jesus. From his global travels and encounters with impoverished believers, Platt learned and often emphasizes the dangers of comfortable Christianity. He posits that, often, affluence can blind believers to the true, sacrificial call of following Jesus. Platt's experiences have solidified his conviction that the Gospel compels a radical re-evaluation of personal priorities, especially regarding wealth [3].

4. **Pastor Timothy Keller**:

As the founding pastor of Redeemer Presbyterian Church in New York City, Timothy Keller has often interacted with both the wealthy elite and the struggling urban populace. His teachings, especially as detailed in his book "Counterfeit Gods," revolve around the concept that wealth, among other things, can become an idol that distracts from a genuine relationship with God. From his pastoral experiences, Keller has discerned that the heart's idols aren't always obvious; they can often be hidden beneath layers of rationalization and cultural acceptance. His insight is that true freedom comes from recognizing these idols and realigning one's heart towards God [4]

From the author:

Thank you sincerely for taking the time to journey through the pages of this book. Your pursuit of understanding and growth, especially in the realm of finances, is commendable. As you reflect on the insights and teachings shared, my heartfelt prayer is that God takes control over your finances, guiding you towards decisions that not only bless you but also those around you. May your financial journey be one that deeply aligns with divine principles, ensuring that your treasures on earth have eternal significance.

Steven Anthony Spencer

RESOURCES AND FURTHER READING:

There's a rich array of religious texts and interpretations when it comes to biblical financial principles. Below is a list of some of these primary sources, along with key interpretations that have been made from them:

1. **The Bible (NIV)**:

 - **Old Testament**:

   - **Proverbs** – A collection of wise sayings, many of which pertain to wealth, poverty, lending, and other financial matters.

   - **Deuteronomy 15:7-11** – Discusses the importance of generously lending to the poor and not being hard-hearted or tight-fisted.

   - **Leviticus 25** – Describes the Year of Jubilee where debts are canceled, and slaves are set free.

 - **New Testament**:

   - **Matthew 6:19-24** – Jesus teaches about not storing up treasures on earth and serving God rather than money.

   - **1 Timothy 6:10** – Paul warns that the love of money is the root of all evil.

   - **2 Corinthians 9:7** – Emphasizes giving cheerfully.

2. **"The Law of Financial Success" by Edward E. Beales** – This early 20th-century text emphasizes the divine laws governing prosperity.

3. **"The Treasure Principle" by Randy Alcorn** – An exploration of biblical views on money and eternity, focusing on the idea that storing up treasures in heaven brings lasting joy.

4. **"Money, Possessions, and Eternity" also by Randy Alcorn** – A comprehensive study into what the Bible says about financial stewardship.

5. **"Rich Christians in an Age of Hunger" by Ronald J. Sider** – This challenges Christians to reconsider how they approach wealth and poverty, making a compelling case for reducing inequality and aiding the poor.

6. **"God and Money: How We Discovered True Riches at Harvard Business School" by John Cortines and Gregory Baumert** – This offers a revolutionary perspective on money, based on the authors' personal experience and an in-depth study of biblical truths.

7. **"The Total Money Makeover" by Dave Ramsey** – While not exclusively a religious text, Ramsey integrates biblical principles throughout his guide on financial management and debt-free living.

8. **"Business for the Glory of God: The Bible's Teaching on the Moral Goodness of Business" by Wayne Grudem** – This investigates business and its potential to glorify God, discussing topics like ownership, productivity, employment, and commercial transactions.

These resources, amongst others, provide profound insights into biblical financial principles, emphasizing ethical earnings, generosity, avoiding debt, and the transitory nature of worldly riches.

ADDITIONAL SOURCES:

[^1^]: Warren, Rick. "The Purpose Driven Life: What on Earth Am I Here for?". Zondervan, 2002.

[^2^]: Collins, Kenneth J. "John Wesley: A Theological Journey". Abingdon Press, 2003.

[^3^]: Platt, David. "Radical: Taking Back Your Faith from the American Dream". Multnomah, 2010.

[^4^]: Keller, Timothy. "Counterfeit Gods: The Empty Promises of Money, Sex, and Power, and the Only Hope that Matters". Penguin Books, 2011.

The Truth on God's Perspective on Being Wealthy

Thank you sincerely for choosing to invest in this book. Your decision today marks the beginning of a transformative journey. As you delve into these pages, be prepared for a paradigm shift in your understanding of finances. I am confident that by the end of this read, your approach to wealth and financial stewardship will be revolutionized, ensuring that your financial life will never be the same again. Embrace the change, and let the journey begin!

"For the love of money is a root of all kinds of evil. Some people, eager for money, have wandered from the faith and pierced themselves with many griefs."

www.ingramcontent.com/pod-product-compliance
Lightning Source LLC
Chambersburg PA
CBHW071459150726
48000CB00006B/2633